DISASTERS IN HISTORY

THE HINDENBURG DISASTER

by Matt Doeden

illustrated by Steve Erwin, Keith Williams, and Charles Barnett III

Consultant:

Eric Brothers

The Lighter-Than-Air Society

Capstone
press

Mankato, Minnesota

Graphic Library is published by Capstone Press,
1710 Roe Crest Drive, North Mankato, Minnesota 56003.
www.capstonepub.com

Copyright © 2006 by Capstone Press, a Capstone imprint. All rights reserved.
No part of this publication may be reproduced in whole or in part, or stored in a
retrieval system, or transmitted in any form or by any means, electronic,
mechanical, photocopying, recording, or otherwise, without written permission of
the publisher. For information regarding permission, write to Capstone Press,
1710 Roe Crest Drive, North Mankato, Minnesota 56003.

Library of Congress Cataloging-in-Publication Data
Doeden, Matt.
    The Hindenburg disaster: / by Matt Doeden; illustrated by Steve Erwin, Keith Williams,
and Charles Barnett III.
    p. cm. (Graphic library. Disasters in history.)
    Summary: "Describes the events of the Hindenburg airship disaster"—Provided by publisher.
    Includes bibliographical references and index.
    ISBN-13: 978-0-7368-5481-8 (hardcover)
    ISBN-10: 0-7368-5481-9 (hardcover)
    ISBN-13: 978-0-7368-6876-1 (softcover pbk.)
    ISBN-10: 0-7368-6876-3 (softcover pbk.)
    1. Hindenburg (Airship)—Juvenile literature. 2. Aircraft accidents—New Jersey—Juvenile
literature. I. Erwin, Steve. II. Williams, Keith, 1958 Feb. 24– III. Barnett, Charles, III. IV. Title.
TL659.H5D64 2006
363.12'465—dc22   2005032286

Art Director
Jason Knudson

Graphic Designers
Jason Knudson and Jennifer Bergstrom

Production Designer
Alison Thiele

Storyboard Artist
Bob Lentz

Colorist
Kristen Denton

Editor
Angie Kaelberer

Editor's note: Direct quotations from primary sources are indicated by a yellow background.

Direct quotations appear on the following pages:
Page 11, from the *Hindenburg* disaster files, Federal Bureau of Investigation, http://foia.fbi.gov/foiaindex/hindburg.htm
Pages 14, 16, 19, 21, from the description of the crash of the *Hindenburg*, National Archives Sound Recording, Herbert Morrison reporting, 1937

TABLE OF CONTENTS

On May 3, 1937, three men approached the *Hindenburg* at the Frankfurt Airfield in Germany. The men were Captain Max Pruss, First Officer Albert Sammt, and Second Officer Heinrich Bauer. They were preparing for a journey across the Atlantic Ocean to Lakehurst, New Jersey. The trip was scheduled to last three days.

It's a remarkable ship. I've captained it before, and I'm still impressed every time I see it.

Even from here, the ship's size is amazing!

It makes me proud to be German. Who else could build an airship so grand?

The German airship was the largest of its kind. Rigid airships, known as zeppelins, were a growing form of air travel at the time. Large passenger airplanes weren't yet in service, so zeppelins were the only way large groups of passengers could travel by air.

Before the flight, 14-year-old cabin boy Werner Franz helped passengers to their rooms.

Are you sure this ship is safe, Werner? How can such a big thing float in the air?

Don't worry. The Hindenburg has made more than 60 flights. It's filled with hydrogen gas. That makes it lighter than air.

All the passengers and luggage are aboard, sir. It's almost eight o'clock.

Prepare for launch.

5

Attention, passengers. I'd like to review the safety rules. This ship is inflated with hydrogen, a flammable gas. We can't have any open flames on the ship!

These ocean headwinds are strong. They're really slowing us down.

We may have a bigger problem, sir. The German Embassy in Washington received a letter warning of a bomb aboard.

Oh, we get bomb threats all the time. The German government isn't popular with some people these days. Don't worry.

8

Ernst Lehmann, a longtime airship captain who was on the *Hindenburg* as an observer, helped calm worried passengers.

Sir, Captain Lehmann here can assure you that we're perfectly safe.

Captain, I'm not going to feel safe until my feet touch the ground.

You don't need to worry, my friend. Zeppelins never have accidents.

This flight has been so smooth. Somehow, I expected more excitement. I'm almost disappointed.

. . . excitement is the last thing I want.

Speak for yourself—we're riding in a big balloon across the ocean . . .

9

CHAPTER 2
ARRIVAL IN AMERICA

On the morning of May 6, the ship approached the U.S. coast. Passengers gathered around the windows.

I see it! Through the clouds, I can see the city.

The ship reached Boston, Massachusetts, around noon.

The ship was scheduled to land at the Lakehurst Naval Air Station in New Jersey. Radio reporter Herbert Morrison and his engineer, Charles Nehlsen, set up their equipment at the airfield.

I thought there would be more reporters here.

A flight like this isn't big news anymore. There's not even anyone really famous on board. It should be pretty routine.

Meanwhile, thunderstorms had sprung up around the east coast of the United States.

Captain Pruss got a transcript of a radio warning from Lakehurst.

Conditions still unsettled. Recommend delay landing until further word.

11

The *Hindenburg* floated over New York City around 3 o'clock in the afternoon.

I don't like this weather. We may have to delay the landing even more, and our schedule is tight already.

Yes, we have a new load of passengers to pick up tonight. Many of them need to be in England for King George's coronation on the 12th.

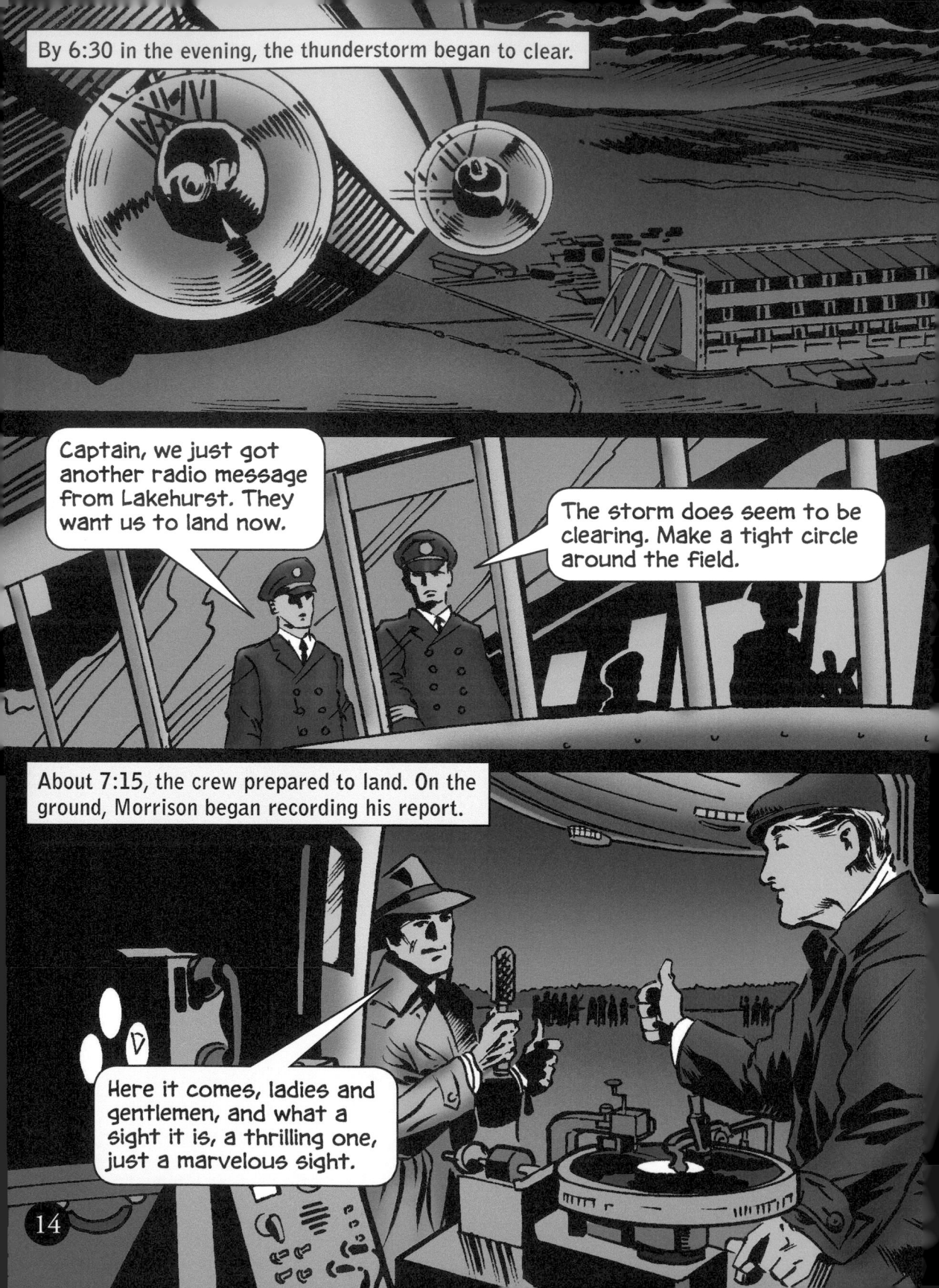

Release the bow landing lines and take it down slowly.

The civilians and U.S. Navy members who made up the ground crew rushed in to secure the ropes.

In an instant, the ship's hydrogen cells began to erupt in flames.

In the control car, Captain Pruss and his officers felt the ship lurch forward.

What was that?

The ship is burning!

Werner Franz was cleaning up after his supper when the ship burst into flames.

I have to get out of here!

Open the windows!

Jump!

It's too far! We're trapped!

Below, people watched in horror.

Chief Petty Officer Frederick "Bull" Tobin told the ground crew to keep doing their jobs.

Oh, the humanity and all the passengers screaming around here! . . . It's—I can't talk, ladies and gentlemen.

Navy men stand fast!

21

CHAPTER 4
ESCAPE

Werner knew he had to act quickly to escape the doomed ship. But as he was running, the ship tilted. He lost his footing.

Above, a water tank burst. The water helped Werner stay conscious and protected him from the heat.

COUGH

GASP

Help! Is anyone there? I can't breathe!

Pruss and Sammt were the last to jump.

Pruss saw radio operator Willy Speck on the ground.

Speck, can you hear me? I'm coming!

Sir, there's nothing more anyone can do. It's over.

Ninety-seven people were aboard the *Hindenburg*. Amazingly, 62 of them survived. But 36 people died in the disaster, including one ground worker. The crash was the first commercial airship disaster. It marked the beginning of the end of airship travel.

MORE ABOUT THE HINDENBURG

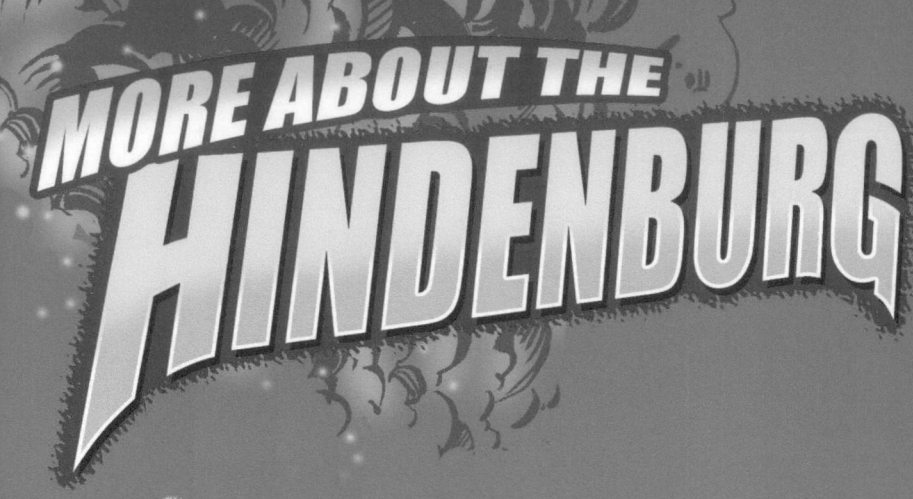

- Zeppelins were named for airship designer Count Ferdinand von Zeppelin, a former German Army officer. Zeppelin had the idea to use a rigid metal frame and cloth outer cover to enclose a group of separate balloons, or gas cells. Many of the great airships followed Zeppelin's design.

- The *Hindenburg* was 804 feet (245 meters) long and held 72 passengers. The cost of a round-trip flight was $720.

- Only 34 seconds passed from the time the *Hindenburg* caught fire to the time it smashed into the ground. Passengers and crew had almost no time to save themselves. Most died from burns.

- Captain Ernst Lehmann escaped the burning wreckage but died from burns the next day.

- No one ever proved what caused the disaster. Many people think it may have been a spark from static electricity in the air. Others suggest that there was a bomb on board the ship. Another idea is that when the ship's landing lines hit the ground, they grounded the electrically charged airship and caused a spark to jump to the ship.

- The *Hindenburg* disaster all but ended the use of hydrogen-filled commercial airships. Airplanes soon took over as the preferred method of air travel.

- Each year, the Navy Lakehurst Historical Society holds a memorial service on May 6 at 7:25 in the evening at the crash site to honor those who died in the accident.

- At the time, most radio stations broadcast only live news reports and entertainment. Morrison's report became one of the first recordings of an event ever to be broadcast.

- After the disaster, ship designer Hugo Eckener felt deep guilt about using hydrogen in the ship's gas cells. He wrote that the disaster would never have happened if he'd used helium. But at the time, many people in the United States were worried about Germany's Nazi government. The U.S. government wouldn't sell Eckener the helium because of concerns that Germany would use zeppelins for military purposes.

GLOSSARY

flammable (FLAM-uh-buhl)—able to start on fire easily

helium (HEE-lee-uhm)—a colorless, lightweight gas that does not burn

hydrogen (HYE-druh-juhn)—a colorless, lightweight gas that burns easily

landing lines (LAN-ding LINES)—ropes used to handle an airship near the ground

zeppelin (ZEH-puh-lin)—a large, cigar-shaped airship with a rigid frame and separate gas compartments known as cells

INTERNET SITES

FactHound offers a safe, fun way to find Internet sites related to this book. All of the sites on FactHound have been researched by our staff.

Here's how:

1. *Visit www.facthound.com*
2. Type in this special code **0736854819** for age-appropriate sites. Or enter a search word related to this book for a more general search.
3. Click on the **Fetch It** button.

FactHound will fetch the best sites for you!

READ MORE

Currie, Stephen. *Escapes from Manmade Disasters.* Great Escapes. San Diego: Lucent Books, 2004.

Deady, Kathleen W. *The Hindenburg: The Fiery Crash of a German Airship.* Disaster! Mankato, Minn.: Capstone Press, 2003.

Sherrow, Victoria. *The Hindenburg Disaster: Doomed Airship.* American Disasters. Berkeley Heights, N.J.: Enslow, 2002.

BIBLIOGRAPHY

Botting, Douglas. *Dr. Eckener's Dream Machine: The Great Zeppelin and the Dawn of Air Travel.* New York: Henry Holt, 2001.

Botting, Douglas, and the editors of Time-Life Books. *The Giant Airships.* The Epic of Flight. Alexandria, Va.: Time-Life Books, 1980.

Dick, Harold G., and Douglas H. Robinson. *The Golden Age of the Great Passenger Airships, Graf Zeppelin & Hindenburg.* Washington, D.C.: Smithsonian Institution Press, 1985.

Flynn, Mike. *The Great Airships: The Tragedies and Triumphs: From the Hindenburg to the Cargo Carriers of the New Millennium.* London: Carlton Books, 2002.

INDEX

They continued for 36 straight hours, resting no longer than five minutes at a time.

The men climbed through passes between towering mountains and crossed jagged glaciers.

On the dawn of May 20, the three men lumbered into the whaling station. People were shocked to see them.

Who are you?

My name is Shackleton.

Where have you been for the past year and a half?

It's a long story, but first, my men need rescuing.

Meanwhile, on Elephant Island, Wild tried to keep up the men's spirits. He woke them every morning by saying . . .

Get your things ready, boys, the boss may come today.

But after four months, they struggled just to get out of their sleeping bags. The men were wet and cold. They also suffered from a poor diet, consisting mostly of seal and penguin meat.

Then on August 30, 1916 . . .

Ship O!

Wild, there's a ship!

More about

Ernest Shackleton

 Ernest Henry Shackleton was born February 15, 1874, in County Kildare, Ireland. His parents were Abraham and Henrietta Shackleton. Shackleton was the second of 10 children.

 In 1901, Shackleton left on his first trip to Antarctica. The National Antarctic Expedition was led by British naval officer Robert Falcon Scott. Scott and Shackleton attempted to find a way to the South Pole. They fell short of their goal by 450 miles.

 On April 9, 1904, Shackleton married Emily Dorman. They had two sons, Raymond and Edward, and one daughter, Cecily.

 In 1907, Shackleton led an expedition to reach the South Pole. He came within 97 miles of his goal. Shackleton turned back because he and his men were nearly out of supplies. Even though he failed to reach the South Pole, Shackleton was considered a hero for trying. The British king knighted him Sir Ernest Shackleton. Shackleton published a book, *The Heart of the Antarctic*, about his expedition.

In 1911, Robert Falcon Scott and Norwegian explorer Roald Amundsen led separate expeditions to reach the South Pole. Scott was not trained to use dog sleds. He and his men pulled, or "man-hauled," their sleds full of supplies. Amundsen was a skilled dog sled driver. By using dog sleds, he was able to travel twice as fast as Scott. Amundsen reached the South Pole on December 14. Scott and his companions arrived a month later. They died during their return trip from the Pole.

 In 1914, as Shackleton's expedition was about to set sail, fighting broke out in Europe. Great Britain and France went to war with Germany and Austria-Hungary. Shackleton offered the service of his ship and crew to Winston Churchill, who later became British prime minister. But Churchill told Shackleton to go on with his expedition.

 In 1921, Shackleton left on what would be his last expedition. While staying on South Georgia, he died of heart failure January 5, 1922, at age 47. He was buried on South Georgia.

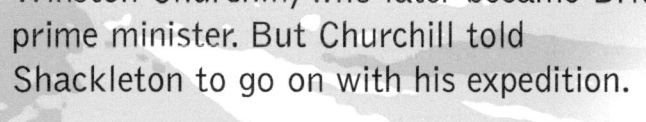

Glossary

endurance (en-DUR-uhnss)—the ability to withstand hardships

expedition (ek-spuh-DIH-shuhn)—a journey for purpose of exploration or scientific research

floe (FLOH)—a sheet of floating ice

pemmican (PEM-mi-kuhn)—a mixture of dried meat and fruit

pressure ridge (PREH-shur RIDG)—ice floes that have been upturned from the pressure of pushing against each other

Internet Sites

FactHound offers a safe, fun way to find Internet sites related to this book. All of the sites on FactHound have been researched by our staff.

Here's how:

1. *Visit www.facthound.com*
2. Type in this special code **0736854827** for age-appropriate sites. Or enter a search word related to this book for a more general search.
3. Click on the **Fetch It** button.

FactHound will fetch the best sites for you!